SHELTER

KATRINA DUNBAR

(SERIES EDITOR: ROB ALCRAFT)

Heinemann
LIBRARY

First published in Great Britain by Heinemann Library
Halley Court, Jordan Hill, Oxford OX2 8EJ
a division of Reed Educational and Professional Publishing Ltd

OXFORD FLORENCE PRAGUE MADRID ATHENS
MELBOURNE AUCKLAND KUALA LUMPUR SINGAPORE TOKYO
IBADAN NAIROBI KAMPALA JOHANNESBURG GABORONE
PORTSMOUTH NH CHICAGO MEXICO CITY SAO PAULO

Produced by Plum Creative (01590 612970)
Printed in China

01 00 99 98 97
10 9 8 7 6 5 4 3 2 1

ISBN 0 431 02750 1

British Library Cataloguing in Publication Data
Dunbar, Katrina
Shelter. - (Taking Action)
1. Shelter - Juvenile literature
I. Title
361.7'632

Acknowledgements

The publishers would like to thank the following for permission to reproduce photographs:
J. Carstairs p19; ChildLine p26 lower; C. Farndon p25; I. Jackson p26 upper; D. Kurlansky pp10-13 all, p27 all, p28 both; Liverpool Post and Echo p15 lower; Mansfield Community Development Project p19; R. Morton p4, p9, p24; Post Studios Ltd p8, pp22-23 all; P. Stewart p6, p14 left, p21; Trip/W. Steer p18; J. Walter p5, p29; A. Wiard p14 right, p15 upper, pp16-17 all.
Cover photograph reproduced with permission of Shelter.

Cover illustration by Scott Rhodes.

Every effort has been made to contact copyright holders of any material reproduced in this book. Any omissions will be rectified in subsequent printings if notice is given to the publisher.

All words in the text appearing in bold like **this** are explained in the Glossary.

CONTENTS

WHAT'S THE PROBLEM?

If you live in a town or city, you have probably seen people huddled in blankets or sleeping bags in shop doorways. They will have woken up stiff with cold. They may not know where their next meal will come from or when they will next sleep in a bed. Thousands of people in Britain spend many nights with no choice but to sleep on the streets. It is these people we usually think of when we think about homelessness.

▼ **Thousands of people sleep on the streets every night. They may end up begging for money to buy food. Finding a job is very hard for homeless people because looking for places to stay leaves less time for job-hunting and they have no address where employers can write to them. Many people will not give a job to somebody who is homeless because they do not believe they will be reliable.**

Nearly half the teenagers sleeping on the streets were once in children's homes.

Lots of families waiting for a real home have to spend months or years staying in other places such as bed and breakfast hotels. Even a family with several children may have to stay in a one-bedroom flat.

Yet there are hundreds of thousands more people, too many to imagine, who do not have a proper home. Some families have to live in a house that is too small. Families and people on their own of all ages may have to stay somewhere in a **hostel** instead of having their own home.

People become homeless for lots of reasons. If you lose your job you might stop being able to pay for your house.

There may not be room for you to stay at home once you have grown up. You may have too many arguments at home to carry on living there.

But the reason why there are so many homeless people in this country is that there are not enough homes which are the right size, in good repair and affordable for everyone who needs them.

5

In Britain today there are over a million homes which are unfit to live in.

SHELTER THEN AND NOW

In the 1960s it would have been rare to see someone sleeping on the street, even in London. The big problem in those days was the standard of homes. Shelter was launched in 1966 to bring housing problems to everyone's attention and appeal for money to improve things.

PUBLIC APPEAL

The Times newspaper gave a whole page to Shelter's first advertisement. The response from the British public showed how much it cared – £50,000 flooded into its tiny new London headquarters in the first month. Over £3 million was raised over the next three years, which was three times the target sum. It would be worth £25 million in today's money.

▶ **An advertisement in *The Times* newspaper the day after Shelter was founded in 1966. It was the first time a charity had used this method to tell the public about the terrible conditions some families had to live in. The money raised by the advertisement was used to improve many homes.**

▼ **Thirty years ago there were large *slum* areas in big cities, like Glasgow and Liverpool, where people lived almost as they did in Victorian times. Many families had no hot water and only an outside toilet.**

Illness caused by bad housing costs the National Health Service an extra £2 billion every year.

✦HOME SWEET HELL✦

Shelter helps over 100,000 families and individuals every year.

WHAT DOES SHELTER DO?

Shelter combines giving practical help with campaigning for change. In 1970 Shelter opened its first **housing aid centre** to give free advice to people with housing problems or with nowhere to live at all. At the same time it talked to the **government** to try to improve people's rights to a decent home.

CAMPAIGN

One **campaign** was for young people – especially 16 to 18-year-olds – who had just lost their rights to **benefits**. Homeless teenagers wrote diaries about how they could not survive without the money they used to be entitled to. Seventeen-year-old Sean, for example, wrote: 'I slept on friends' floors until I ran out of friends, then slept behind an old school gym for a few weeks until my legs were so stiff from the cold that the doctor said I was risking permanent damage to them.'

HELPING PEOPLE

Sean eventually moved into a one-bedroom council flat with Shelter's help.

It is for people like Sean and homeless people of all ages that Shelter was set up 30 years ago. This is also why it still exists today. There are now housing aid centres spread throughout England, Scotland and Wales. In England, centres help over 100,000 homeless or badly housed people every year.

A GROWING CHARITY

Shelter has grown enormously from a handful of people to over 300 staff and volunteers. Now, for example, there is a team the size of a school class whose job is to raise the money Shelter needs to carry out its work.

46,000 children woke up in a temporary home this morning.

These people each do different jobs: Helen (far left) raises money and Louise (far right) talks to the *press*, Margi gives advice to homeless families. Linda and Tarn (middle) work on campaigns talking to the public about homelessness and Shelter's work.

Many homeless young people end up sleeping in the streets. Shelter has centres where they can get help with claiming benefits and with finding a home. At the same time it campaigns to improve things for everyone in his situation.

People sleeping on the streets are often attacked by passers-by at night.

MEET THE LANGLEYS

I'm Gareth Langley and I am nearly 10 years old. We have our own home now, but we were homeless for nearly a year and had to live in several bed and breakfast hotels, which I hated. Staying in this sort of hotel can be a treat, but it wasn't for us, because we had no space and had to leave our toys and things with friends.

I had to share a bedroom with my older sister, Paula, who's 18, and my mum and dad. It was our living room as well as our bedroom – we only had one room for everything and I had nowhere to go if I wanted to be by myself.

We had to share the tiny kitchen downstairs with eight other families. Where we were last Christmas, we carried our turkey and the whole Christmas dinner up three flights of stairs to our room to eat!

This is one day when we were still living in a bed and breakfast hotel.

The Langley family now have a new home, which Shelter helped them to get. They talked to the council lots of times on the family's behalf to persuade them that this family needed a proper home urgently.

Mrs Langley, Paula, Gareth and baby Lauren leave the bed and breakfast hotel to look for a new home.

Living in damp houses gives children breathing problems.

> Mrs Langley and Gareth look at the advertisements in the estate agent's window. All the houses are too expensive or too far away from Gareth's school. Gareth wants to move back to the area where most of his friends live and where he can go fishing.

8.00am I'm too tired to go to school today. I find it hard to go to sleep while everyone else is watching the telly, so I often don't get to sleep until about 11 o'clock. Yesterday I fell asleep during my favourite class.

9.00am Dad has gone out to see someone who may have a new job for him. Mum has been waiting to go downstairs to make breakfast because it gets too crowded before 9 o'clock in the kitchen. Someone has stolen our eggs, so I'm annoyed that I can't have a boiled egg.

9.30am Paula, Mum and I try not to spend too much of the day in our room because it drives us mad being cooped up together all the time. We're looking after my other sister's baby, Lauren, today.

10.00am Mum and I go to the estate agent to look for a house we can rent. Mum spends most days walking around all the estate agents. I have lived in three different places in two and a half years and can't keep track of where most of my toys are anymore.

1.00pm We didn't find a house this morning, but Dad has good news back at the bed and breakfast. He's got a new job, so he takes us to the new drive-in McDonalds to celebrate.

2.30pm I spend the afternoon playing with the spaceman I got from McDonalds and watching TV.

> It's a rare time of celebration for the Langleys. Mr Langley has been looking for a new job for several months. He hurt his back badly in his last job and can no longer do the same kind of work. Luckily, he now has at least three months of work, which means the family can buy some new clothes at last.

It can cost £1000 just to move house.

MEET JANE FILBY

CASEWORKER

My name is Jane and it is my job to help and advise people who come to this Shelter **housing aid centre** in Plymouth, Devon. Most of my days are like this one.

8.30am I try to get to the office an hour before we open to the public in order to catch up with my paperwork.

9.20am The phone rings and it's the father of the family I'm representing in **court** later on this morning. Mr Coleman lost his job eight months ago and cannot afford to pay for the family home anymore. He is very worried that the court will take their home away from them.

9.30am Mrs Ashley and her grandchildren arrive for their appointment. About one in every four people who walks through this door is having a problem with renting their house. Mrs Ashley and her husband have suddenly had their rent put up. I go through the letter I wrote to their **landlord** before we opened today. It explains that he cannot put the rent up without giving a few weeks' warning.

◀ **Mrs Ashley needs Shelter's help because her landlord has put up the rent by £20 each week with no warning. The Ashleys want to stay in their home, but they cannot afford to pay the extra money and have had no time to save up for it.**

12

200 families' homes are taken away in court every working day.

◀ Jane goes to the county court to see if she can stop the bank from taking the Coleman family's home away from them. If they lose their home, the family will have to move into a *hostel* which is 13 km from the children's school. This would mean paying bus fares they cannot afford, or moving school.

10.15am Time for a quick cup of coffee and to catch up with the other two **caseworkers** before I dash off to court.

10.50am I get to the county court on time. The bank, which lent them the money to buy their house, agrees to give them another six months to pay off some of the money they owe. Phew, what a relief!

12.30pm A couple of telephone calls about other cases and a snatched sandwich before I go off for my afternoon's training about the new housing laws that have just been created by the **government**. They will affect the advice I give people like the Ashleys and the Colemans, so the training is an afternoon well spent.

5.00pm I head home straight from the training course, full of new knowledge and pleased that the Colemans are safe in their home, for now at least.

▶ **Shelter caseworkers have training whenever new laws are passed, so that they will be up to the minute with the advice they give to people.**

There are nearly 50 Shelter housing aid centres.

MEET CHRIS HOLMES

SHELTER'S DIRECTOR

My name is Chris and I run Shelter. I spend a lot of my time travelling all over the country to talk about homelessness and what Shelter does. I have meetings with all kinds of people, from the Prime Minister's special advisers to pop stars who want to use their fame to help us raise money.

As Shelter's director, it's up to me to make sure that everyone in the organization is working towards the same goals. I plan our work into the future. Train journeys can be good 'thinking time' if my mobile phone doesn't ring too often.

This year it's Shelter's 30th anniversary and we're holding some important events to tell the public about homelessness. This is the day we launched our 30th anniversary and had our birthday conference.

5.45am Today starts very early for me because I am on breakfast TV at 6.25 this morning to talk about Shelter's 30th anniversary.

10.00am Reporters from radio, TV and the newspapers interview me just before the conference.

▲ **A TV crew come to the conference to interview the director for the lunchtime news programme. Millions of people will watch the news later, so it is important to speak well in front of the camera.**

14

Chris appeared on 94 different TV programmes on this one day.

10.30am The conference begins and I tell the 100 or so people there about families like the Halls, who are sitting beside me. Daniel Hall is only four years old. He cannot understand why he and his mother cannot live with his father. We learn that it is because the only job Mr Hall could find was a day's travel away from home. The council, from whom the family rent their home, will not help them to move to where the job is. So Daniel only sees his father about once every month. I feel sad and angry as I tell the story.

12.00am I rush straight to the station to catch a train to Liverpool, where we have a centre to help young people with housing problems.

3.30pm Down by the Liverpool docks on the River Mersey, I release balloons to represent the number of local homeless people. It makes a wonderful scene above the water.

5.00pm I am just closing my eyes on the train back to London when my mobile phone rings with the best news of the day — the Hall family will be able to live together very soon. Following our conference this morning, their council have agreed to help them to move.

▲ **Chris speaks to the audience about the problems of homelessness in Shelter's 30th anniversary year. Susan Hall tells how Daniel offered to give up sweets if he could see his father more often.**

▼ **The afternoon is spent in Liverpool, releasing balloons as a reminder of how many people are homeless in Liverpool. This picture was in the *Liverpool Post* and *Echo* newspapers the next day.**

Hundreds of families in England have to live apart because one parent works far away from home.

MEET TARN LAMB

CAMPAIGNER

I'm Tarn and I'm a Shelter campaigner. As well as helping families to find homes, Shelter tries to improve the situation for everybody who is homeless now or who may find themselves homeless at some point in the future.

At Shelter we talk to the **government** and others whose job it is to decide on homeless issues. We discuss whether to build more homes or give other kinds of help, such as money, to people who are struggling to keep a roof over their heads. At the same time we tell the public about homelessness and what we think needs to be done. An important part of my job is organizing events around the country so we can meet people who may want to **campaign** with us for more homes.

This is the day I organized a public meeting for our 30th anniversary.

8.00am I get to the office early to put together folders with information on our campaigns.

9.30am Dominic, one of the other campaigners, helps me put posters up around the hall where we're holding the meeting.

▲ Tarn and Dominic put a banner up outside the meeting hall. It's a good advertisement for the charity and may bring in some passers-by who didn't receive an invitation or see the article about the meeting in the local newspaper.

Eight out of every ten letters an MP gets is about homelessness or housing.

The actress and TV presenter Margi Clarke was homeless herself when she first moved from Liverpool to London.

2.30pm Back at Shelter's headquarters. I catch up with a colleague who spent yesterday evening at a meeting with some **Members of Parliament**.

10.30am Everyone who is speaking at the meeting has now arrived and I take the chance to talk to our **celebrity** speaker, Margi Clarke.

11.00am The hall is getting full. I'm pleased to see so many familiar faces.

1.00pm Lots of people wanted to talk about how they could help with our campaigns after the meeting, which is the best sign that it went well.

5.30pm The day ends with planning the next public meeting, which we sent out invitations for last week.

Tarn gives people information packs as they arrive for the meeting. This means they can telephone her in a few days' time if they have any more questions about what they hear today. Or they may want to help with a letter-writing campaign to Members of Parliament.

Pop stars such as East 17 give concerts to raise money for Shelter.

WORK IN THE COUNTRY

Being homeless in a town or big city is hard. Being homeless in the country is even harder.

In the country there are hardly any **hostels** or **housing aid centres**. For homeless people who live in remote places there may only be a bus once every few days to get them to the nearest town for help. In the country it is harder to find work. One choice is to pick fruit and vegetables during the summer, and then move to the nearest town during the winter.

COAL-MINING VILLAGES

Some villages only exist because there is work in the area. When the work goes, so do the people. For example, several pit villages in Nottinghamshire depended entirely on coal mining. When the mines closed a few years ago, many villagers had to leave their homes to look for jobs elsewhere.

◀ **Farmwork is badly paid and hard work, but it may be the only work people can get in the country. Even though it costs less to live in the country than in a city like London, the difficulty of getting around and the lack of jobs makes life tough if you are poor.**

Over half the people sleeping on the streets in England are outside London.

HOW SHELTER HELPS

Shelter opened **temporary** centres in church halls in two ex-mining villages. This was to help families stay in their homes or to find new homes nearer to where there might be work.

Shelter housing aid centres in rural areas are a long way from some people who need help. These centres put more time into advising people over the telephone or by post. **Caseworkers** may even drive out to visit families with emergencies who live in very isolated areas.

This Nottinghamshire village has many run-down houses because of the mine closure. Some families have split up because of the strain on the parents of having no work or money, and their neighbours and friends slowly moving away. There are no places to work and even in the nearest town there are not enough jobs to go round.

Nearly three-quarters of a million homes are empty in England.

WORK WITH POLITICIANS AND THE PRESS

▼ **Coachloads of Shelter supporters, young and old, came to London on 24th October 1995 to talk face-to-face to their MP about changes to laws which are important for homeless people.**

10,000 people wrote to the government to protest before the new 1996 Housing Act was passed.

POWER OF PERSUASION

Members of Parliament, known as MPs, have a lot of power. It is the MPs in **government** who run the country and make decisions which affect all our lives. The government decides, for example, how to tackle homelessness. Shelter keeps MPs up-to-date by discussing with them what is going on in the **housing aid centres**. Through discussion with MPs it tries to persuade the government to spend more money providing more and better homes.

▼ **Many children helped Shelter to launch the 'Homelessness Costs' campaign. Homeless children have great difficulty finishing their schooling because they move schools so often or have nowhere to do homework. So homelessness costs children a good education.**

ON TV

The government has made new laws stating how people will be helped with finding a home. The Housing Act of 1996 means that people will only have help to find somewhere **temporary** to live. Shelter was very worried that this would make life tougher for homeless people. So the **campaigns** team organized 1000 Shelter supporters to come from all over the country to **protest** against the laws and to meet their MPs at the Houses of Parliament. The **demonstration** was on the national TV news.

The protest was part of the 'Homelessness Costs' campaign. For this campaign a cardboard house was made and **press** photographers were invited to take pictures of children with the campaign message. The campaign pictures were in lots of newspapers the next day. This meant that even those MPs who hadn't spoken directly to Shelter still heard about the campaign and the demonstration against the new laws.

21

Children can miss whole terms of school because of homelessness.

WORK TEACHING ABOUT HOMELESSNESS

BARNSTORMS

Shelter holds many public meetings called **Barnstorms**. At these meetings Shelter tells people more about homelessness in their area. These are important for getting new people to help with **campaigns**. It also makes people more aware of the most common housing problems, which they or their family or friends may need help with in the future.

AVOIDING HOMELESSNESS

Shelter workers also give talks at school assemblies, or to youth groups. Some schools devote a whole lesson to learning about homelessness. Shelter teaches them how to avoid ending up homeless. This involves proper planning before leaving home and making sure they have enough money to pay for somewhere to live. Children who leave home in a hurry after a row are the most likely to end up homeless.

22

Shelter has information packs for school children of all ages.

> Sixth-formers cast their votes to decide the winner of a debating competition about homelessness. The real ballot box is to remind everyone about the importance of voting in the *general election*, which you can do once you reach 18.

◄ A Shelter campaigner talks to a group of teenagers about homelessness so that they can get some tips on how to avoid becoming homeless themselves, and also understand better why Shelter campaigns for homeless people.

SIXTH-FORM DEBATE

As part of Shelter's 30th anniversary celebrations, a conference was organized where sixth-formers competed in a debate about what the **government** should do about homelessness. A real **ballot box** was used to vote for the teams in the debate. One of the team members said she couldn't believe that 16-year-olds got less money in **benefits** than 18-year-olds – even though their living costs were the same.

▲ Homelessness is now a subject on the school curriculum and some classes will do a piece of work on what they have learned from Shelter's visit. This is a seven-year-old child's idea of what it means to be homeless.

23

Most young people do not know what their rights to housing and benefits are.

WORK WITH SPECIAL PROJECTS

As well as trying to help whoever comes through the doors of a Shelter **housing aid centre**, Shelter has to tackle particular emergencies. Some of the housing aid centres have developed projects to solve problems that are common in their own area.

YOUNG PEOPLE

Many Shelter centres run projects to help young people find homes. The Liverpool centre has made a study with other organizations in the area to find out how many young people are homeless, and what type of place would best suit them to live in. For example, the project workers talked to groups of young people about whether shared houses or one-bedroom flats are more suitable.

▲ Shelter found flats for these young people to share. Shelter helped them to get all the *benefits* they had a right to receive.

Under 18-year-olds may only get training instead of benefits.

This project is now being extended to the whole country, with special project workers in three regions. The project will continue over the next three years and is being paid for with a donation from Midland Bank.

EMERGENCY HELP

Shelter runs a special project with the charity Crisis during the coldest months of winter. Emergency **hostels** are set up in schools or church halls to prevent people from having to sleep out in temperatures which are below freezing.

▼ An old man leaves his tent of polythene on a cold winter morning. Every winter people die from sleeping outside in temperatures below freezing. Emergency beds and hot food save lives.

People on the streets often die before they reach the age of 45.

LONDONLINE

Dick Whittington came to seek his fortune in the City of London, where the streets were supposed to be paved with gold. Today, people of all ages still leave their home towns to escape an unhappy life, or to look for a new job and a better life in London. Many of them find themselves with no job and no money, and quickly run out of friends' floors to sleep on. That's when they may telephone Shelter's LondonLine service for help.

Caseworkers on LondonLine can tell when up to three people are waiting to get through, by buttons lighting up on the wall.

OPEN ALL HOURS

LondonLine's night-time service was set up five years ago because people desperately needed emergency help at night when everywhere else that offered help was closed. Now it is open 24 hours a day and a team of **caseworkers** gives advice to people ringing from all over London. LondonLine has a special number which means that the call is free even from a phone box. The caseworker may give advice to one caller about how to make sure a **landlord** mends a leaking roof he promised to mend months ago. The next caller may be looking for a **hostel** to stay in.

► ChildLine and LondonLine are emergency telephone helplines which teenagers can ring at any time of the day or night. The number of children on London's streets is growing at a rapid rate.

LondonLine gets about 100 telephone calls every night.

BED BOOKINGS

LondonLine's computer will tell the caseworker which hostels still have empty beds. Often the caller will be in a phone box in the centre of London and will have to travel to the other side of London to get a bed for the night. Sometimes there are no beds left anywhere, and people have to sleep on the street. The best Shelter can do then is to tell them where there will be a van giving out food.

IMMEDIATE HELP

Trish recently rang LondonLine. She was 16 and had been thrown out of her London home by her parents when she was 15. Her parents had then moved abroad. Trish had been staying with a series of friends, but had finally outstayed her welcome and rang Shelter in a panic at about seven o'clock on a Friday evening. The caseworker rang the local **social worker**, who agreed to find Trish somewhere to live because of her age. He couldn't help until Monday morning because he was already dealing with two other emergency cases, so LondonLine found Trish a place at the Centrepoint emergency hostel.

LondonLine is open 24 hours a day, every day of the year. It is the only London-wide free telephone advice service and still gets about a third more calls coming into the **switchboard** than caseworkers can pick up.

▼ Crisis is another charity which sends vans out late at night to parts of London where there are a lot of homeless people. Crisis workers give out hot food and drinks, and clothes and blankets.

▲ Teenagers can stay for up to two weeks in this emergency hostel run by the charity Centrepoint. They may have come out of a children's home or have run away from their family.

Most people ringing LondonLine need somewhere to sleep.

VISION OF THE FUTURE

Gareth Langley has got his bicycle and toys back from the attic where they were stored while his family were homeless. He is looking forward to the future. Shelter will continue to work for all homeless children, like Gareth.

HOPE FOR THE FUTURE
Homelessness will only stop being one of the biggest problems in this country if we build more new homes and repair old ones. Everyone has the right to a home where the children can do their homework in peace and have somewhere to play and where there is room for all the family.

GOODBYE TO THE PAST
If more homes are built, then in the future nobody should have to put up with becoming ill because of sleeping in a bedroom with damp walls. Nobody should have to move house and change school three times in one year. People who grow old sleeping on the streets should become a thing of the past.

▶ Building new homes is one way to stop so many people ending up homeless. Building homes also means more jobs for builders, which helps them to pay for their own homes.

Every year fewer new homes are built with government money.

◀ Gareth Langley plays in the park near his new home. Six months ago he had nowhere to have friends back for tea and nowhere quiet to play or do homework. Now he has his bike back and the future looks bright.

▲ Shelter will continue to *campaign* until we live in a country where everybody has somewhere to call home, which is warm and safe, which they can pay for and which is near school and work.

At least 100,000 extra homes to rent are needed every year in the UK.

FURTHER INFORMATION

If you would like to know more about homelessness and Shelter's work, telephone or write to our Information section. We have fact sheets on a variety of topics you have read about in these pages – on young people, for example. We can help you with general facts and figures on homelessness. We have posters and information to help with school projects.

If you would like to help Shelter raise money, telephone or write to our Community Networks Fund-raising section. We can give you ideas for sponsored activities, such as swims and bike rides. We have packs to help you have lots of fun with different ways of raising money at your school. We even have a pack to use carol-singing at Christmas.

You may want to wear a T-shirt like the one shown here, to show your support for Shelter. You can buy this, and also Christmas cards and presents from our **Shelter Trading Catalogue**.

You can write to all these sections of Shelter at:
88 Old Street
London EC1V 9HU
Tel: 0171 505 2000

If you have a problem with homelessness yourself, you can ring us on the same telephone number.
If you live in the London area, telephone LondonLine, free of charge, on 0800 446441

Other useful organizations, which you have read a little about in this book, are:

Centrepoint
Bewley House
2 Swallow Place
London W1R 7AA
Tel: 0171 629 2229

ChildLine
2nd Floor
Royal Rail Building
Studd Street
London N1 0QW
Tel: 0171 239 1000 Helpline: 0800 1111

Crisis
First Floor
Challenger House
42 Alder Street
London E1
Tel: 0171 377 0489

GLOSSARY

ballot box a large metal box where people put pieces of paper on which they have put their vote. The box is opened after everyone has put a vote in, and all the votes are counted to decide the winner.

barnstorm a day of campaigning in one town or city which usually ends with a big public meeting about homelessness

benefits regular money payments given by the government to people who are poor

campaign a series of activities with the aim of bringing about change, for example a campaign for more homes. Someone involved in a campaign is called a campaigner.

caseworker someone who helps homeless or badly housed people by talking to them and giving advice

celebrity a famous person, often an actor or pop star

court a place where a judge makes decisions if two people or companies want different things, or when somebody has broken the law

demonstration a group of people coming together to show how strongly they feel about something

general election the time, once every five years, when everybody in the country over the age of 18 votes for which political party they want to run the country

government this is the team of people who have been elected to run the country. They decide how much money is spent and on what, and how much tax people pay.

hostel a shelter, usually with dormitories like a boarding school, where people can stay if they haven't got a home

housing aid centre an office where people can go for help and advice if they are homeless or have problems with paying for their home

landlord someone who owns a house or flat and lets people pay to live there

Members of Parliament people who are elected to represent a particular part of the country

press the group name for journalists, who write in newspapers or for radio or TV

protest complain or show anger about something, or call for a situation to be changed

slums houses which are poor and where nobody wants to live

social worker someone who works for the local council and helps people with their problems, especially very young or elderly people

switchboard a machine where lots of telephone calls can be answered at once by one person and then passed on to whoever each call is for. They are used in hotels and offices and anywhere where a lot of people ring in at the same time.

31

temporary for a short time

INDEX